DEALING WITH YOUR EMOTIONS AS PARENTS

The Key to Positive, Effective Parenting

Deborah L. Belcher

Table of content

Chapter 1

How to handle your emotions as parents

Research shows that when guardians respond cruelly and with profound power, youngsters' pain will in general rise, and the issue is less inclined to get settled. Here are a few methodologies that can help.

Meander any jungle gym or shopping center, and eventually, you are probably going to notice a parent training her kid to take full breaths in and out to quiet herself, or guiding her to "utilize her words" as opposed to hitting, kicking, or snatching. These are for sure great nurturing techniques for assisting youngsters with figuring out how to oversee and communicate their feelings in sound ways — a basic yet difficult undertaking — that I tended to in a past article, which brought about many remarks by guardians to the tune of: "It's dealing with our feelings that is the large problem positive" nurturing throughout our children's lifetimes is our mindfulness and self-guideline as guardians.

Nurturing small kids (truly, offspring of all ages) is a seriously profound encounter. There is the unadulterated joy of nestling, playing, chuckling, investigating, and taking pleasure in your child's day-to-day development and disclosures.

And afterward, there are the difficulties, the snapshot of stress,outrage, disappointment, and disdain at not understanding what a child's cry means and how to quiet her, at the unreasonable requests of a little child, or at the forceful way of behaving of a more established kid toward another child. These encounters normally inspire unmistakable inclinations that can be difficult to deal with. Yet, the vast majority of the ways of behaving that we find rankling are a characteristic piece of growing up and are not planned to be malignant; they are a youngster's work to adapt to a troublesome inclination or circumstance. Kids need our help, not our resentment.

So it means a lot to check out and deal with our sentiments since what we respond to at these times profoundly means for our youngsters' capacity for self-guideline, poise, and by and large close to home well being far into what's in store.

Examination (and reality) shows that when guardians respond cruelly and with profound force, kids' misery will in general rise and, whatever the central concern, it is doubtful to get resolved. Here are a few techniques that can help:
Tune into your feelings
Check out your sentiments.
Sentiments are not set in stone – they simply are. It's how we manage them that can be useful or terrible. At the point when you escape the matter of passing judgment

on your sentiments, you can be more open to checking out and possessing them-the most important phase in controlling and communicating sentiments in helpful ways. One father so expressively summarized it, going directly to the main concern: "It's critical to figure out how to perceive your triggers. It's unreasonable to anticipate that your youngsters should manage your stuff."

All of us are human. The uncommon parent wouldn't be consumed with shame, immediately followed by outrage and hatred at a kid, when, for instance, at some family occasion she has a tantrum for not getting the primary piece of cake, while her charming cousin is enchanting everybody by assisting with distributing the cuts and taking the final remaining one, so unselfishly, for herself.

Checking out your sentiments permits you to settle on a cognizant choice — rather than an automatic response — about how best to answer. For this situation, it could mean taking a few full breaths to clear your head, then serenely let your kid know that you realize she is disheartened, yet it's impractical to constantly go first and that she will be ok imparting trust in her capacity to adapt. Albeit resisting the urge to panic is difficult to work, the advantages are sweeping and the settlements reach out far into what's to come.

Resisting the urge to panic permits you to remain associated with your kid as opposed to expanding her pain by encountering a profound break with you; she feels comprehended, not disgraced, which makes her more open to tolerating the cutoff being set; and when you respond smoothly, it diminishes the pressuring chemical in her mind, which helps her quiet more rapidly. Remaining even-tempered likewise brings about significantly less regret for having let go completely, and numerous fewer evenings hitting the hay feeling like all you

did that day was holler and weigh on your children – a typical and difficult experience for some guardians.
Do the unforeseen.

At the point when each bone in your body is pushing toward blast at some ludicrous interest or provocative way of behaving, it tends to be exceptionally successful for your kid (and you!) to give her a major loving squeeze or accomplish something senseless. This can diminish the pressure and strain of the circumstance, and accomplishing something startling can likewise end the undesirable way of behaving.

This isn't pampering or surrendering. If your kid is letting you know, he loathes you since you won't allow him to have 5 additional minutes to play (and he hasn't completed his game yet! he simply needs 5 MORE MINUTES!) and you approach him with a giant squeeze while saying, "It seems as though you want a major mom embrace," you are telling him you hear his dissatisfaction and feel for it. You are not giving him five additional minutes – which would be "pampering" or safeguarding him from being required to adapt as far as possible he could do without. It might astound you how this can change the tides – doing something contrary to what he expects when he is in provocative mode. Or on the other hand, don't answer his "lure" and simply turn on the music and begin to do a senseless dance, the entire way to the supper table you are attempting to change him too.

Essentially say, "Go along with me," and move along. It might sound corny, yet it tends to be exceptionally powerful – and again ease the two his pressure and yours. Give yourself a break.

At the point when you are struggling with resisting the urge to panic within the sight of your kid, be certain your kid is protected (which could mean placing him in a pack 'n' play for a couple of moments) and allow yourself a little while to chill off. You could say: "Mother needs an opportunity to contemplate how I can best assist you."

This can be an extremely strong procedure in that it messes up the cycle, which can at times stop the kid in his tracks. What's more, it permits you to stay present even notwithstanding the pessimistic profound power these circumstances frequently stir. It additionally fills in as an exceptionally strong job demonstrating to your kid how to oversee compelling feelings – precisely the thing you are attempting to educate. This gets you out of a receptive state and allows you to contemplate the significance of your kid's way of behaving and what you believe that he should gain from the experience.

It's substantially more possible you will concoct a reaction that draws the line or guides your kid's way of behaving while at the same time remaining supportive.

This procedure can be particularly strong when utilized along with your companion or accomplice, particularly when you are in conflict about how to answer your kid: "Mom and Daddy need to have a little pow-wow to contemplate how we can assist you with this test." This sends a significant message to your kid, past demonstrating discretion, that you are a smart nurturing group and are cooperating to assist him with figuring out how to adapt.

Overseeing solid pessimistic feelings is without a doubt a lot not exactly simple or easy. In any case, it merits the work, because the result is tremendous, for yourself as well as your kid. As one wise parent put it: "How you respond to things is how they'll figure out how to respond to things.... You must be in charge of yourselves if you believe that they should be in charge of themselves."

Emotion

What are Emotions?

Feelings will be sentiments. To begin to comprehend your feelings, you want to pose yourself two inquiries:

How would I feel?

How would I be aware?

Yet, others likewise have feelings. Simultaneously as monitoring your sentiments, you likewise should know about those of others.

You likewise need to inquire:

How would others feel, and how would I be aware?

There are multiple ways that we can perceive how others are feeling, yet, especially by seeing what they say, and how they act, including their non-verbal communication. Research recommends that over 80% of correspondence is non-verbal, implying that it comes from non-verbal communication and looks. A large number of us could do without discussing our feelings, particularly not on the off chance that they truly make a difference to us, so they will generally be communicated much more in our non-verbal communication. See our page on Non-Verbal Communication for more.

Feelings and the Brain

Feelings are not deliberately controlled. The piece of the cerebrum that arranges feelings is the limbic framework. It's believed that this piece of the mind developed genuinely almost immediately in mankind's set of experiences, making it very crude. This makes sense of why a profound reaction is frequently very clear, yet at the same exceptionally strong: you need to cry, take off, or yell.

This is because these reactions are based on the need to make due.

Feelings are unequivocally connected to memory and experience. Assuming something awful has recently happened to you, your profound reaction to a similar improvement is probably going to be an area of strength for me.

Infants feel feelings, yet can't be guaranteed to reason. Feelings are likewise firmly connected to values: a close-to-home reaction could perceive that one of your key qualities has been tested. See our page on Dilts' Logical Levels for more about this.

Understanding this connection to memory and values gives you the way to deal with your close-to-home reaction. You're close to home reactions don't be guaranteed to have a lot to do with the ongoing circumstance or reason, yet you can defeat them with reason and by monitoring your responses

Assisting your child with dealing with their feelings expects you to figure out how to deal with yours first.

Why Becoming Your Child's Emotion Coach Begins by Managing Your Own Emotions First

In case of a plane crisis, travelers are encouraged to get their own breathing devices first, before helping other people. The explanation they're approached to do so is that individuals unfit to inhale (or the oblivious people) are of little assistance to other people.

"Putting your breathing apparatus first" additionally applies to numerous areas of nurturing. It's hard to be a decent parent when you're overpowered, disappointed, and feel a little skeptical about your nurturing decisions. It's likewise challenging to be a decent parent while you're battling with your feelings.

Feeling guideline studies stand out enough to be noticed throughout the long term. Unfortunate feeling guideline abilities have been connected to various pessimistic results, including poor actual wellbeing. Stifling feelings have additionally been connected to cardiovascular infections and asthma. Albeit the outcomes are as yet uncertain, a few investigations have likewise tracked down ties between poor close-to-home guideline abilities and mental issues.

We presently realize that what we converse with kids about feelings means for their social, scholarly, and mental prosperity past the youth years. We additionally know that before we can help children to direct their feelings, we should figure out how to deal with our feelings. For example, the proof recommends that uneasiness-inclined guardians are substantially more liable to give their tensions to their children.

We likewise realize that children advance more from watching us than they do from paying attention to us. At the point when we give them the right structure, we give them the fundamental apparatuses to deal with their feelings

Things to remember to assist you with managing your feelings.

1. Talk is cheap

Showing kids how to deal with feelings isn't tied in with smothering those feelings. It's tied in with showing your kids that feelings exist, yet they can be made due. Your child pays attention to you about how she ought to respond to serious areas of strength like resentment and uneasiness.

2. Offer another person guidance

Profound guideline studies allude to the inclination to zero in on possible arrangements as circumstance adjustment. It implies trying to adjust what is happening to modify its effect. For instance, conversing with your accomplice about something he does that influences you can assist with persuading him to change, or possibly be more aware of what his activities mean for you.

Taking on a third-individual viewpoint to assess a feeling initiating an occasion can make it simpler to manage that occasion. While you're battling with a specific circumstance, envision that it's occurring to another person. What might you encourage that individual to do?

3. On the off chance that you can't retaliate, escape

Choosing to skirt an occasion you realize you'll loathe is a typical feeling guideline procedure. This is generally alluded to as circumstance choice, and it implies drawing closer or staying away from specific circumstances, submits, or individuals to control one's feelings. For example, before a significant meeting, you could decide to call a hopeful companion as opposed to investing energy with a cynical one. On the off chance that dental specialists have consistently made you restless, having another person take your child to a dental arrangement might assist you with directing your feelings.

However, emotional guidelines aren't just about diminishing pessimistic feelings. Drawing on different investigations, he contends, for example, that a modest individual can diminish uneasiness by keeping away from social circumstances, yet this can offer transient alleviation and possibly lead to social seclusion.

4. Check out the circumstance through open-minded perspectives

Mental change alludes to adjusting how we judge our ability to deal with feeling-evoking circumstances. A portion of the normal methodologies incorporates disavowal, separation, the reappraisal of circumstances, or endeavors to decipher occasions more.

We frequently manage feelings by reappraising them (changing how we view circumstances) or smothering them. While it is as yet indistinct which techniques work best, Gross' investigations have shown that smothering feelings diminishes pessimistic as well as good feeling expressive ways of behaving. Besides, smothering feelings little affects pessimistic encounters. As such, reappraising circumstances is bound to prompt helpful outcomes.

5. Concentrate somewhere else
Redirecting your consideration from feeling inspiring circumstances can assist you with overseeing compelling feelings. Attentional sending incorporates techniques like interruption, i.e., zeroing in consideration the non-profound parts of a circumstance, and focus, i.e., picking exercises to distract from the triggers.

At last, assisting your child with dealing with his feelings expects you to figure out how to deal with yours first.

Quiet is a feeling of interior poise that allows us to work overall quite well. It is the ideal condition of the cerebrum, upheld by a body aligned with it, permitting us to tackle our intellectual abilities while keeping an offset with our feelings. At the point when you are quiet, you are in your zone, unperturbed by interruptions or pain.

The cerebrum has complex frameworks for unwinding and quiet to neutralize its components for sharpness and nervousness. These body-based instinctive frameworks lie not inside our cerebrums, our level headed higher mind, the seat of rationale and thinking, but our center mind, which controls our feelings and motivations, and the huge ecological sensor and container that is our body.

A quiet body is a quiet psyche. Not the reverse way around, as a great many people accept. At the point when a mother shares with her child, "Tony, kindly quiet down," she is utilizing a hierarchical way to deal with quieting her youngster – requesting that he utilize a sane, cognizant interaction to calm down. Then again, assuming that a mother shares with a shouting kid, "Break!" and sits him in a seat confronting a wall, that is involving a granular perspective – calming his body to accomplish a feeling of quiet.

Meander any jungle gym or shopping center, and sooner or later you are probably going to notice a parent training her kid to take full breaths in and out to quiet herself, or guiding her to "utilize her words" as opposed to hitting, kicking, or snatching. These are to be sure great nurturing methodologies for assisting youngsters with figuring out how to oversee and communicate their feelings in solid ways — a basic yet difficult errand — that I tended to in a past article, which brought about many remarks by guardians to the tune of: "It's dealing with our feelings that is the huge issue." Indeed, this has been my own most noteworthy nurturing challenge, as it has been for the many guardians I have worked with.

I'm decidedly persuaded following 30 years of training that the absolute most significant expertise for "positive" nurturing throughout our children's lifetimes is our mindfulness and self-guideline as guardians.

Nurturing small kids (truly, offspring of all ages) is a strong close-to-home insight. There is the unadulterated joy of snuggling, playing, giggling, investigating, and having a great time with your child's everyday development and disclosures. And afterward, there are the difficulties — the snapshots of stress, outrage, dissatisfaction, and disdain — at not understanding what a child's cry means and how to quiet her, at the nonsensical requests of a baby, or at the forceful way of behaving of a more established kid toward another child. These encounters normally summon unmistakable inclinations that can be difficult to deal with. However, a large portion of the ways of behaving that we find irritating are characteristic pieces of growing up and are not planned to be malignant; they are a youngster's work to adapt to a troublesome inclination or circumstance. Youngsters need our help, not our resentment.

So it means quite a bit to check out and deal with our sentiments since what we respond to at these times profoundly means for our youngsters' capacity for self-guideline, restraint, and generally close-to-home well-being far into what's in store. Exploration (and reality) shows that when guardians respond brutally and with close-to-home force, kids' trouble will in general heighten and, anything the main concern, it is doubtful to get settled.

At the point when you are struggling with resisting the urge to panic within the sight of your kid, be certain your kid is protected (which could mean placing him in a pack 'n' play for a couple of moments) and allow yourself a little while to chill off. You could say: "Mom needs an opportunity to contemplate how I can best assist you." This can be an extremely strong technique in that it messes up the cycle, which can some of the time stop the kid in his tracks. Furthermore, it permits you to stay present even notwithstanding the pessimistic close-to-home force these circumstances frequently excite. It likewise fills in as an extremely strong job displaying for your kid how to oversee compelling feelings – precisely the thing you are attempting to educate. This gets you out of a receptive state and allows you to contemplate the importance of your kid's way of behaving and what you believe he should gain from the experience. It's substantially more logical that you will concoct a reaction that draws the line or guides your kid's way of behaving while at the same time remaining sustaining.

Overseeing solid gloomy feelings is doubtlessly a lot more difficult than one might expect. Be that as it may, it merits the work, because the result is immense, for yourself as well as your youngster. As one wise parent put it: "How you respond to things is how they'll figure out how to respond to things. You must be in charge of. ourselves assuming you maintain that they should be in charge of themselves.

Chapter 2

Step-by-step instructions to Deal with Stressed and Overly Emotional Parents

Shuffling work, bringing up kids, running a family, and being an individual from the local area can be difficult work and frequently puts a great deal of weight on guardians. This pressure can be very effectively passed to their children, making the family strained and unsteady children. You might be a youngster or teen who needs to manage worried guardians, which can be troublesome.

You may likewise work in childcare, training, or are an adolescent consideration specialist, and there will be times when you should manage profound and focused guardians. It might appear to be overwhelming from the start, but with a touch of work, it tends to be finished. There are a few rules you can continue to limit struggle, relate, and work decisively with your own or others' folks in a helpful manner:

Managing Your Parents

1. Manage the circumstance. Assuming your folks are excessively personal or focused, it is by and large more straightforward to deal with the circumstance rather than take part in it. Assuming you want to get something explicit from them or converse with them about something explicit, attempt to be immediate with your inquiries or inside your conversation. If you try not to answer profoundly, your folks might be bound to answer likewise. Regardless of whether they are, you will be more averse to acquiring pressure from the collaboration on the off chance that you simply endeavor to oversee them as opposed to taking part in their profound, focused conduct.
For instance, assuming your folks are raising their voices at you, don't raise yours

back. Smoothly attempt to proceed with the discussion without exacerbating it.

2. Remove yourself from the circumstance. On the off chance that your folks are excessively anxious and you can't deal with it, eliminate yourself from the discussion or circumstance, if conceivable. Assuming that your folks are worrying you, go to your room or one more space in the house. Try not to do it in an ill-bred manner, however, attempt to eliminate yourself from the circumstance so you don't exacerbate it or become focused on yourself due to their excessively profound way of behaving.
On the off chance that you are in a circumstance where you can't move away from them, attempt to eliminate yourself from the discussion.should be possible by letting them know that you would rather not talk, deferentially letting them know that you are eliminating yourself from the discussion, or essentially overlooking any

focused on or profound conduct they display in your presence

3. Help the circumstance. If you see what is causing the pressure or profound conduct in your folk's lives, attempt to assist with it if possible. There might be a few circumstances where you can't help, like private matters with their relationship or their associations with others, or at times cash inconveniences, however, there are different circumstances where you can help. In any event, eliminating only a tad of the tension can help de escalate the circumstance to where your folks might quiet down.

For instance, if you see that an untidy house is making your folks worry, have a go at getting around the house or washing the dishes. Or on the other hand, if you are mature enough to find a new line of work, get a new line of work and begin getting your very own portion of things or providing your folks with a tad of cash to assist with things

4. Talk to them about it. On the off chance that your folks are excessively anxious and profound for you to manage, converse with them about it. Have substantial instances of how they have acted that have worried you or been excessively close to home. Try not to fault or blame them for their awful way of behaving, simply clear up for them that they have been excessively close to home and focused on recently and that it is slowing down your life. Most guardians may not understand how they have been acting or the ability it is affecting you.

Ensure you do this smoothly. Regardless of whether your folks retaliate with brutal words or can't understand what they've been doing, ensure you remain mentally collected. You can unfortunately do a limited amount a lot in these circumstances. Whenever you've told them, it depends on them to transform it. If it doesn't change after some time, take a stab at having the discussion again with extra instances of their activities.

5. Listening to the Parents

Support the guardians. Guardians today have a great deal to fret over. Bringing up youngsters while shuffling the wide range of various requests of life in the present economy and culture can unquestionably cause significant damage. Guardians can get overpowered and, as an overseer of their kids, you give help to them and their pressure too. Youth work is about collaboration, and aiding support guardians is helping support their youngsters. It tends to be exceptionally useful for guardians to have somebody they trust and who has genuine information about their youngster simply stand by listening to them talk.

Some of the time everything you can manage to help worried guardians is to give a place of refuge to them to move their feelings out into the open and to give them the help they need.

6. Pay regard for the guardians. There are certain strategies you can utilize, other than basic help, that will assist you with effectively paying attention to guardians when they converse with you. Whether you are on the telephone or face to face, plant your feet solidly on the ground and stay present. Keep your breathing quiet and engaged, incline into the discussion, and show up for the parent. Remain as grounded as conceivable in your collaborations with them so you can remain as zeroed in as conceivable on their discussion.

To make a place of refuge, you must be a protected individual who is focused and seriously viewing their interests. Be available for them. The guardians will see assuming you truly participated in what they are talking about. If you are truly drawn in, you can deal with their need to cleanse their feelings and stresses.

7. Take notes. Another undivided attention procedure is to take notes. If you are not on the telephone, inquire as to whether they mind on the off chance that you take notes. Make sense of that you simply need to ensure you are completely retaining what they are talking about so you can work with the remainder of your group to assist with finding answers for their interests and assist with removing a portion of the weight from them. This will tell them that you care about their interests and their kid also.

8. Make intelligent proclamations. Now and again when guardians are excessively personal, it may very well be hard for them to keep on track. Use articulations like that beginning with things like, "What I am hearing you say is," or, "I can hear from your voice how focused you are." These assertions will tell them you recognize their pressure.

You can likewise involve approving explanations, for example, "That should be truly troublesome" to help the guardians genuinely comprehend you are tuning in and taking their pressure, feelings, and concerns genuinely.

9. Let them realize you are here to help. At times individuals are awkward when they get pushed. The guardians may likewise find it trying for them to feel so close to home and need to try not to look for help. Guarantee the guardians that you are there to help, you are there for their kids, and you are there for them. Tell them it is an aspect of your responsibilities to offer help and inquire as to whether there is anything you can do to cause them to feel happier with talking and articulating their thoughts.

10. Legitimize the parent's concerns and concerns. Try not to offer exhortation, limit the guardians' pressure and feelings, or propose any sort of handy solution. The initial step is to tune in and let the parent express whatever they might be thinking,

start to finish. Attempt to abstain from intruding on them while they are portraying their issues to you. Keep in mind that they are the guardians, and regard that their involvement in their youngsters might be unique to your experience as an educator or parental figure.

By keeping judgment and arrangements, you can more deeply study the relational peculiarities, different parts of the kid being referred to, and ways of behaving that may not be present in everyday schedule care. By utilizing your listening time to likewise assemble data about the kid, the guardians, and relational peculiarities, you will have a superior munitions stockpile of thoughts of how might benefit from some intervention the guardians and kid.

11. Comfort the guardians. While you are tuning in after you reflect on the parent how vexed and focused they sound, urge them to attempt to inhale and unwind. This will

assist with dissolving what is happening and set the guardians straight.

By building up that they are in good company and you are effectively tuning in, you can help de-raise the parents close to their home state so you can more readily help them.

Approving the Parent's Feelings

Console the guardians. Sound, intelligent exhortation, and arranging is perfect, however when you feel anxious and overpowered, more often than not you need to be heard and feel approved. After this, you can contemplate the issues that you are managing. Remember this while you are managing worried guardians. Genuinely focusing on them too as approval and consolation can go far in bringing down the profound power so arrangements can ultimately be talked about.

Continue to promise the guardians that you esteem their concerns and feelings.

Pose intelligent inquiries. Intelligent inquiries are questions that begin with why, what, who, or when. Attempt to stay away from questions that are highly contrasting or just yes or no. Intelligent inquiries approve of the experience the guardians are having.

It additionally makes it simpler for you as the audience to accumulate as much data about what is the deal with the parent and start to think about potential arrangements. Intelligent inquiries likewise permit the parent to investigate their sentiments and why they are anxious.

Some of the time talking through an unpleasant time with somebody the parent feels is an expert can truly assist the parent with feeling upheld

Attempt questions, for example, "How might I assist with everything going on?" or "What precisely do you believe is causing this issue for your kid?" These require long, top to bottom reactions that the guardians can reply to. These inquiries will likewise assist you with sorting out the specific issue and sort out how to fix it.

Approve what is happening. Keeping down all judgment centers around the way that the sentiments the guardians are having are genuine for them. Offer expressions that approve of their feelings. Approve that being a parent overall too is so troublesome. Approving the parent and their feelings can likewise assist with quieting the parent down. Assuming you feel like somebody is paying attention to you and understanding you, it assists you with feeling not so much cautious but rather more open to discussing choices and arrangements.
Let them know something like, "I figure out your dissatisfaction with everything going on," or, "I can see the pressure and upset that this occasion has caused you."

Relate to the parent's sentiments. Permit yourself to feel what the parent is feeling and attempt to imagine their perspective. People have an extraordinary capacity to understand others, and if you are working in childcare or youth work, you probably know all about how much sympathy can be intended for someone else. The guardians that are anxious, close to home, and connect to assist with requiring your compassion as well. Recall that adolescent work is truly family work, and by feeling for what the parent is going through, you are supporting the parent, yet you can likewise identify with the kid and their home circumstance.

Even though you are not at the arrangement stage yet, by really sympathizing with the parent, you can start to shape inquiries of your own about what you would do in that particular situation, which will assist you with making an activity plan. Keep those inquiries in your sub-conscience and remain fixed on tuning in, approving, and sympathizing with the parent.

Guarantee that you are here to help. At the point when guardians get excessively pushed, it tends to be truly useful for them to realize they are in good company, and that different grown-ups are here to help them. You are in an expert position and address somebody who they believe they ought to have the option to entrust with their kids. Make plainly that they are in good company and that you are tuning in.

This will assist with approving their sentiments and show that you understand them so you can be strong. Let them know that this is an aspect of your responsibilities that you are prepared to do.
Guarantee the guardians with expressions, for example, "I'm here to assist you with each worry you have," or, "I comprehend your dissatisfaction and I am here to help you until you are happy with the outcome.
Recommend breathing activities to assist with destressing the guardians. Assuming you have listened mindfully, as of now,

approved, and related the parent you are managing is lashing out and heightening their feelings, delicately recommend that you both take part in profound relaxation. Regardless of whether you are on the telephone with a parent, request that they put a hand on their paunch and inhale profoundly into it. Express to them that you are doing profound breathing excessively to assist with dispersing the inclination and stress. Likewise, let them know that you need to be quiet and focused to the point of aiding them.

Try not to rush this step. Permit a lot of time for the guardians to vent and talk, yet in addition, acknowledge when now is the ideal time to quiet down and begin being useful.
Be aware of your significant investment too. On the off chance that contemplating arrangements isn't proper because the parent is simply excessively profound, attempt to set up another gathering or call when you can talk once more.

Request direction from the guardians. If you don't know how best to help the guardians, ask them what the most effective way is for you to help them. Give them the power and control, which may likewise assist with facilitating their feelings of anxiety while you are conversing with them. Ask what they need from you at this time to best serve them, their misery, and their kid. This can assist them with centering, feeling supported, and feeling appreciated and like they have a voice.

Attempting Concrete Solutions

Address the issues independently. Begin helping the guardians slowly and deliberately. Realizing that there is help on the way and that you are in their group can assist the parent with having a solid sense of safety and uphold. Contingent upon what the worries are, attempt to address every one of the stressors independently and durably.

For instance, if their kid is carrying on at home, address what should be possible from your side as the guardian or educator, and what the parent can do at home to supplement the activities you are taking when the kid is in your consideration.

Request a rundown of worries. Request that the guardians make a log of the issues and worries that they are having and how the kid is involved. Request that the guardians attempt to see times, occasions, circumstances, and individuals that are causing the pressure and feelings. Along these lines, you can find out about what kinds of administrations and mediations will best fit what is the deal with the family. This exercise can likewise assist you with seeing comparative occasions with the kid when the parent isn't anywhere near.

Give back to the family. On the off chance that the guardians are focused on account of lodging, monetary, or monetary worries,

utilize the assets you have locally or work environment to assist with supporting the family through this time. Give the guardians however many choices as you can about administrations, government assistance projects, and school programs for families battling with neediness.
This may not offer a quick arrangement, but rather it can assist with diminishing their pressure over the long haul.

Offer external arrangements for the issues. Assuming there are clear occurrences of family misfortune, misuse, substance maltreatment in the family, or separate, or different stressors that are straightforwardly connected with the recent concerns, be proactive in finding projects and advising that will help the kid. Contact the school advisor for ideas, or ask your boss for references for directing.
Most metropolitan networks have free projects for kids who have been survivors of misuse. As an adolescent specialist, you

ought to approach assets for when family circumstances, for example, injury emerges. Guarantee the parent that you are their ally and will bend over backward to track down the assets to get their kid the assistance they are requiring.

Include the parent and pay attention to their point of view. By fostering a group-like climate, not exclusively will the parent benefit by feeling included and engaged, but the kid will likewise benefit by having various viewpoints and procedures at home too.

Ask the parent straightforwardly about the way that you can help. Keeping the guardians included will assist them with feeling less weak, and thus this will assist with decreasing the sensations of stress and lower the emotionality. Introduce yourself as a piece of their group, and as somebody who needs to help them and thinks often profoundly about the prosperity of their youngster.

Empowering Self Care

Recommend taking care of oneself for the parent's pressure. As anybody will tell you, nurturing is the hardest work you can have. Some of the time, when guardians are focused on and over-profound, it very well may be useful assuming you urge them to take reality to really focus on themselves. By doing this, you are again showing support, showing that you are tuning in, and helping facilitate their pressure by allowing them to zero in on themselves.

Contingent upon the seriousness of the circumstance, you might have to propose various things. For instance, if there has been a misfortune in the family, urge the parent to look for guidance. Propose to interface them with free administrations, or request that the parent contact their insurance agent to find a specialist that can help them. The parent might be past their capacity to completely deal with what is happening in their family, and looking for the assistance of an expert might be ideal for themselves and their kid.

Urge the parent to set aside margin for themselves. Guardians frequently neglect to deal with themselves. Regardless of whether this implies an hour alone in a hot shower without any interference, urge the parent to track down ways of unwinding. You don't need to be unequivocal with your ideas, yet be genuine that you feel they merit some spoiling. Utilizing your sympathy, reaffirm that their pressure and feelings are substantial, and they should deal with themselves so they can likewise deal with their youngster.

Ask the guardians what they need. It could assist you with asking the guardians what they figure they might have to get past their distressing feelings. Check whether there is anything you can do to help, for example, recommending nurturing classes or books.

Contingent upon what is focusing on the kid, maybe a care group would be useful and you can assist them with tracking down it. For instance, if the guardians have a mentally unbalanced youngster and are extended past their limits, a care group for guardians with medically introverted kids may be an extraordinary way for them to free sentiments from seclusion and associate with different guardians with comparative stressors.

Stress the requirement for profound solidness. Present for the guardians how significant their profound state is for the prosperity of themselves, yet in addition to their youngster. In some cases, guardians can lose themselves in the everyday pressure of work and kid-raising, and it tends to be useful to hear that their close-to-home wellbeing is substantial. Let the parent know that they matter, their sentiments matter, and although you care for their kid as your work, part of really focusing on that kid is focusing on the whole family.

Be a mainstay of help and approval for pushed guardians. Over the long haul, better profound well-being in the guardians makes for better close-to-home well-being for the kid. As a young specialist, your responsibility is to advance fields for solid kids. Be caring, tune in, approve, and identify guardians who get pushed.

Instructions to Manage Feelings As Parents

Utilize the recipe: One decision + 8 Feelings + 90 Seconds

The decision is transparency and eagerness to know about and be in contact with however many of your sentiments as could reasonably be expected

Identify one of the 8 sentiments and be available

Allow yourself 90 seconds to comprehend what you are feeling through real sensation

The surge of these sentiments and substantial responses regularly last 60-90 seconds

Notice what you are encountering in your body, endure the substantial sensation and ride the wave to the opposite side of the 90 seconds before responding

For example, the intensity of cheeks flushing from shame

By remaining present to the inclination and substantial sensation you will acquire an understanding of the choice you want to make and the move you need to initiate

Changing Around Your Language As A Parent

Am I? Will I? Will I? Isn't that right?

These cultivate question

Switch those inquiries and rethink them to articulations: I am, I can, I will, I do

These cultivate an encounter of certainty

The most effective method to be a quiet parent

Figuring out how to be a quiet parent is something each parent I know seeks as well. Be that as it may, goodness it truly is exceptionally difficult, right?

Step-by-step instructions to Be a Calm Parent may be something we as a whole need to know however the responses can appear to be slippery

Everyday life can feel like sheer turmoil and can appear constant, confused, and muddled. I think everybody needs a little assistance around here.

Figuring out how to be a calm parent implies figuring out how to comprehend kids don't fathom social guidelines equivalent to grown-ups. Guardians know how to adapt to feelings, and youngsters should be directed, so how about we guarantee we're doing it the legitimate way?

At the point when children enter their baby years, most guardians battle to keep their mental soundness. Baby to even high school years is difficult, without a doubt. It might appear to be difficult to remain even-tempered when amidst fits and control issues, regardless of age.

It is difficult however is do-ready to figure out how to be a quiet parent and there are a ton of useful things we can do to assist ourselves with being more settled today.

Our kids are definitely worth the effort and we deserve it as well. Quiet truly is infectious and we will make a more settled home and more settled connections by simply dealing with ourselves.

Positive reasoning aids so confirm to yourself You realize that how generally will be a quiet parent and you can be one.

Steps on the most proficient method to be a quiet parent - straightforward tips that truly take care of business

I generally think basic hints are awesome. Step-by-step instructions to Be a Calm Parent aren't overly complicated and are not difficult to learn.

The more muddled an issue gets the harder it is to unravel. Quiet is more than anything that has a significant impact on mentality and consideration regarding the association. View these tips underneath on the most proficient method to be a quiet parent and check whether you can set them in motion. You will be so satisfied you did

Planning for progress is how to be a quiet parent

Absence of rest is a tremendous issue
For example, being worn out or lacking rest can set off outrage toward others. Kids know

how to test their folks, and if you are battling with an absence of rest, ask others for help. Having the option to press in rest might be an extraordinary beginning in the mission for how to be a quiet parent

For instance, if you need to realize how generally will be a quiet parent

Try not to plan play dates if you or your kid are excessively worn out if you have a bustling day in front of you.

On the off chance that you have a bustling day in front of you, ensure you get to an early bed.

Some alone time could assist you with loosening up. Ask relatives or recruit a sitter for a couple of hours.

Do attempt to get your rest on target. It very well may be so troublesome on the off chance that you have a head loaded with considerations humming around. Perhaps you could put resources into a diary or some concerned dolls and void your interests before you hit the sack around evening time. A sleep time routine can likewise be enormously useful

How to be a calm parent? Change your demeanor:
Impacting how you approach specific activities is vital to how to be a quiet parent. Not all that your youngster does is an impression of your nurturing. All kids will shout, contend, and test their mental stability. As your youngster develops, so do their advancement abilities and they will require direction en route.

The significant thing to recollect is everything isn't occurring to you, it's simply how you respond.

Attempt to keep even-tempered and steady. You can constantly pick how you answer. A basic interruption might be all you want to allow your feelings to subside and for you to get your reasonable head on - the one that

realizes you don't need to customize everything the one that knows very well How to Be a Calm Parent.
Instructions to be a quiet parent - relax

Have a go at holding up your 10 fingers and envision them to be candles - breathe in, then individually leisurely blog them out, taking a major full breath in again before you blog out everyone.

Presently manage the issue. It is a lot simpler to keep composed when you have managed your breathing and taken a delay as well. Attempt it
Instructions to be a quiet parent-house rules:
Having decisions that your kid comprehends is significant. Ensure that your home is kid protected to guarantee the gamble of injury is brought down. A few instances of rules include:

Assigned places for food and beverages

Assigned den/regions
Instructions to talk with each other
Child safe home
This doesn't make you an edgy parent, what it does is give you a place of refuge that feels quiet and regarded and in which you can loosen up realizing some request is set up. Try not to be terrified of having rules they truly can assist with turning out to be more harmonious.

Assumptions for being a quiet parent
Re-examine your assumptionUnfortunately, this isn't a limited-time offer change. Your kids are continuously developing and promoting being developed, and your assumptions for them will likewise change. It's not difficult to become involved with figuring your kid might be fit for controlling their activities, yet everything should be learned. Kids realize what they see, so show others how it is done.
Having an incredible organizer assists you with figuring out how to be a calm parent

Nurturing is a ton of experimentation. Not all children are something similar, so training and directing will appear to be unique for each situation. Figuring out how to be a quiet parent will make things go a little smoother. As guardians, we surely assist them with growing, yet we need to acknowledge where they are too.

Over to you - do you have any idea how to be a quiet parent?

As consistently I truly do very much want to hear from you, my perusers. How would you cause yourself to feel quieter - might at any point share your thoughts with us please in the remark area beneath. We all need to realize that we will generally be quiet parents and sharing is in every case great.

Instructions to be a calm parent isn't super complicated yet it expects you to consider it

with some concentration and to work on certain propensities essentially.
I'd truly very much want to hear what works for you.

Chapter 3

How to be Calm Even When Your Child is Out of Control

Can we just be real – with regards to the kid-parent relationship, there is one individual who has mature poise and one more modest individual with extensively less restraint.

The outcome is that as a parent, we need to manage ourselves, yet we likewise need to assist our children with directing.

Calm Parenting

Do your children worry you? Do you end up becoming restless when you ponder their way of behaving, and what it could mean for their future? Do your kids have any idea how to "provoke you" and bring you into a contention?

Assuming this is the case, you're in good company. While nurturing has its prizes and delights, it can likewise be debilitating, baffling, and testing. Many guardians want to have a quiet home with not so much clash but rather more getting it.

What's the best method for figuring out how to be a quiet parent? In all honesty, it begins with zeroing in more on yourself and less on your children. You have the most command over yourself and your reaction to a given circumstance.

Tips To Stop Screaming and Start Parenting Effectively

You're a parent, you've likely been there: your kid says or accomplishes something that provokes you, and then before you know it, you're shouting and shouting as loud as possible. Also, they're answering in kind.

Thereafter, you feel depleted, upset, and baffled. You can't help thinking about why it generally needs to boil down to a shouting match.

No Parent Is Perfect – We All Yell on occasion

Guardians must recall that we're flawed, and we can gain from our errors. An occasional shout or two doesn't make you a terrible parent. We all shout at our children on occasion

For what reason Do Parents Yell at Their Kids?

Most guardians shout and shout at their children since they're baffled. At the specific second when you lose it, you don't feel like you have some other choices. It becomes like an automatic response or a trigger being pulled. As such, you don't ponder what you're doing. You simply answer.

Guardians can likewise let their disappointment with their children develop over the long haul. They go from one episode to another without giving results, and the disappointment becomes greater and greater. At last, they break and respond by shouting instead of managing the mischief reliably and really.

Why Screaming at Your Child Doesn't Work
Shouting and shouting at your children sends the message that you're not in charge. Also, if you're not in charge, they could expect that they're in control. It's likewise vital to comprehend that children feel risky and restless when their folks show up wild. These are negative messages to ship off your kid, and it subverts your clout in the family.

I need to make sure that it's OK to talk firmly to kids. Yet, blowing up and afterward tightening up to shouting isn't useful, particularly assuming it's over absolutely everything. At the point when you shout at everything, the shouting loses its impact and has no importance when there's real mischief.

The outcome of nurturing is having a decent outlook on the task you've finished in showing your kid how to act – and you can't feel better about yourself if you're shouting constantly. While ongoing shouting turns into the standard, kids are likewise able to believe it's acceptable for them to shout constantly, as well. Your child discovers that shouting is a reasonable reaction when you're baffled or overpowered. It shows nothing for sure. All things considered, it instructs that life is wild, and you're crazy.

Here is the reality: assuming you use shouting to get your children to agree, you're not showing them better critical thinking abilities. Shouting at an issue doesn't make it disappear. For sure, it normally aggravates the issue. At the point when children are shouted at constantly, they figure out how to endure the shouting instead of progressing their way of behaving. At last, your kid blocks you out and out.

Also, assuming shouting was viable, nurturing would be simple. We'd simply shout at our children, they'd change their way of behaving, and our concerns would be tackled. Yet, we all realize that it is quite difficult.

Tips to Help Parents Stop Screaming at Their Kids

If you wind up shouting at your kid as often as possible, it won't be difficult to stop yourself – essentially not immediately. Figuring out how to have an impact on how you speak with your kid takes practice. You want powerful devices because your children will provoke you to attempt to inspire you to let go completely – which they're utilized to. In any case, you can figure out how to have control and speak with them. The following are six hints that will assist you with refocusing.

1. Try not to Attend Every Fight You're Invited To

"You don't need to go to each battle no doubt about it."

Leaving a shouting match will frequently leave the battle speechless, at that moment. Regardless of assuming the battle is starting, if you're profound into it, or it's been happening for ten minutes, you can prevent and pull back from the circumstance.

Pulling back from the intensity of the circumstance likewise helped me as a parent to sort out what my reaction ought to be. In some cases, it implied investing some energy away from my kid and afterward returning later and managing their troublemaking.

2. Try not to Respond Immediately To Bad Behavior if You Feel Triggered

I believe it's fine to stand by ten minutes or even hold on until the following day to return and consult with your kid about their unseemly language or conduct. Frequently, things with our children are genuinely not so critical. The majority of us shout about things that are minor when you truly consider them. They could feel pressed at that point, yet that is simply because of our tumult, and not really because our child's way of behaving is so terrible.

You can tell your kid:

Your way of behaving isn't suitable, and we will discuss it some other time when things are quiet

It's occasionally really great for a kid to need to ponder what is happening or occurring for some time before you have that discussion.

An extremely straightforward thing you can do is build up to ten while truly separating yourself from the circumstance. So build up to ten, leave, go into an alternate room, and do an alternate action. Regardless of whether you understand what's setting off your disappointment, assuming you realize that you are overcompensating (and shouting is typically an eruption), attempt to separate.

3. Give Yourself Transition Time When You Get Home

It's normal for guardians to battle with their children right when they return home. Regularly, during the drive home, the parent is pondering the battle they will have when they stroll into the entryway. It's very nearly an inevitable outcome.

Subsequently, I suggest that you allow yourself to progress when you return home. Require ten minutes to waste time, accumulate your contemplations, and afterward emerge from your room and converse with your children. They might carry on as they can hardly stand by ten minutes from the start, however, they'll become acclimated to it. What's more, they'll figure out how to ultimately give you your space.

4. Set yourself up Mentally for Situations That Trigger You

Realizing your triggers is significant. We as a whole have triggers, and frequently they're not the most reasonable things. I believe it's helpful for guardians to understand what their triggers sets them off. Is it the feet on the love seat, the sass, or their wreck in the kitchen? Show yourself what you can do when you're setting off to answer all the more actually.

At the point when I was returning from work, I likewise got ready for how I would respond. I would ponder internally, "OK, when I return home, if my child hasn't gotten his work done and assuming he's made a wreck once more, I won't shout or shout. I'm about to allow myself to loosen up, and afterward emerge and manage his way of behaving." So if you know your triggers, you can design your response.

Assuming that you're dealing with remaining in charge, I think you want to take a gander at yourself. Begin auditing what occurred sometime later and attempt to rehearse more successful correspondence with your children where you're not wild. Once in a while having more certain cooperations implies there's less time for the negative.

Request yourself what kind of parent you might want to be. No one needs to be known as the parent who shouts at their children constantly and appears to be crazy. Request yourself what kind of parent you need to be.

What's more, recall, it's rarely past the point of no return — you can begin making these enhancements whenever.

5. Get Support From Trusted Friends or Family If you're attempting to gain more influence and might want to quit shouting, I prescribe that you converse with your life partner or confide in companions and recognize every last bit of it. I don't believe there's anything to be embarrassed or humiliated about practically we all shout. Your mate could have a few experiences or a few thoughts of what you can do. They additionally could see what a portion of your triggers are that you haven't seen yourself.

Be mindful so as not to trust different guardians or relatives who are critical or who express shock or consternation at your nurturing difficulties. These individuals will just exacerbate you about yourself, and that is not powerful.

6. It's Okay to Apologize for Screaming

I would in some cases go over things with my child and apologize for hollering and make sense that I'd had a hard day and that I was sorry I took it out on him.

Assuming you choose to apologize, grasp that there's no need to focus on getting pardoning from your children. Rather, it's tied in with claiming your way of behaving, gaining from the circumstance, and attempting to improve sometime later.

Step-by-step instructions to Keep Calm and Guide Your Child to Better Behavior This Year

Have you been thinking back on the keep-going year, considering how things went with your kid? Provided that this is true, maybe you feel baffled when you ponder their way of behaving and your response to it. Perhaps you feel like regardless of what you do as a parent, nothing changes. In any case, comprehend that positive change can occur in your loved ones. You're not trapped in those negative examples you truly can further develop things, beginning today

As you think back, it tends to be useful to recollect what you wanted for last year close to this time. Perhaps you wanted for an extended time of less battling with your children or envisioned that your kids would turn out to be more dependable and spurred.

Maybe you wanted your disobedient high schooler to transform into a more helpful one, or for your mate to support you more. Perhaps you yearned to when things got tumultuous or wanted to parent from your standards rather than from uneasiness. However troublesome as it very well might be to reflect on occasion (particularly if things didn't turn out how you'd trusted), if you can see last year with interest and perception as opposed to with lament and brutal decisions, you'll have a superior possibility of further developing things now.

It's essential to understand that each relationship encapsulates components of a dance. What's more, there are some incredible dance moves and some that have gone downhill and should be resigned. Do a self-stock by remaining back and noticing yourself as you connect with your kids and other relatives. Ponder your dance moves, and pose yourself the accompanying inquiries:

What is my hit the dance floor with my youngster? Do we continue to have a similar battle?
Which steps in the dance do I have to change? Do I get found out in a fight for control and wind up hollering or yielding?
Regardless of whether it seems like the dance you truly do can't be modified, realize

that you can begin changing those negative examples with your kid at present.

Rehash After Me I am not in charge of my kid's ways of behaving, considerations, and sentiments yet I am in charge of my own.

At the point when we as guardians feel answerable for our kid's ways of behaving, considerations, sentiments, and results throughout everyday life, we profoundly put resources into their way of behaving. We will generally accept that their identity is an impression of us. At the point when guardians have this impression, there is an assumption and strain to shape their children into who they accept they should be; any other way we can't quiet down. We feel tension which prompts reactivity as we endeavor to shape them up. Accordingly, our children then, at that point, respond to us normally with some type of disobedience. That dynamic can add to a disheartening and disappointing power in the family. For what reason is this sort of reactivity so damaging? Since a close-to-home response doesn't prompt learning, critical thinking, goal, or self-bearing not to mention sure association.

Last year was an unpleasant one with your children, odds are this is because you and your children were more responsive to one another. Intense external conditions could have expanded your feelings of anxiety. Constant uneasiness alongside stresses like a demise, work changes or a move, maturing guardians, or disorder increase the opportunity for greater reactivity in the family. Yet, recollect, while we have zero control over numerous things that happen to us, one thing you can assume command of is how you figure out how to answer pressure and trouble in your life.

Quit Reacting and Start Responding

For what reason is it critical to be smart instead of over-respond to your youngster this year, and consistently pushing ahead? Answering is an approach to dialing back, remaining even-tempered, and noting somebody nicely as opposed to letting that automatic response kick in. One method for doing this is by acknowledging you have command over your feelings. Between activity and your response, you have the space to conclude it's ideal to's thought process, feel and answer. You have a decision. You are never completely helpless before another person's way of behaving. So assuming your small kid is moving around on the floor since she would rather not get dressed, don't begin moving with her. All things considered, delay and consider a powerful reaction.

Maybe you'll choose to put your earphones on while she rolls and shouts and manages her sentiments. Or on the other hand, perhaps you'll choose to furnish her with a choice. You can pick which outfit to wear. After you put it on, we'll go to your companion's home. Which one do you pick? Or then again, assuming that your high school little girl is pummeling entryways and feigning exacerbation, don't hammer and move with her. Rather you can discreetly ask her what's disturbing her. Or then again you can try not to draw in with her until she's worked off her steam.

When that's what you hit the "stop" button and pick a viable reaction given your sound standards as opposed to an automatic response, you are accountable for yourself and your connections. At the point when you're responsible for yourself, you won't have to attempt to control your kid or any other person, besides.

By overseeing yourself rather than your kid by getting out of his case and into your own you will have given him the profound space to figure out how to be accountable for himself. Also, he will be adequately quiet to have an independent mind and tackle issues with greater development.

Express These 5 Things and Have a Calmer Year with Your Kids

The following are five comments to yourself that will assist you with keeping composed with your children and will assist with adding to a more quiet and serene year.

I'm not my kid and my kid isn't me. He can act one way and I am allowed to pick how I will act, regardless of how I decide to act.

I can utilize my nurturing values to direct me when my feelings get set off. I'm completely mindful of my way of behaving. My kids can't 'make' me lose it.

I'm liable and responsible for how this year goes. I'm not in charge of how any other person acts or thinks, yet I am completely accountable for how I act and think.

It's unrealistic to 'control' others and attempt to persuade them to be the way I maintain that they should be so I can feel like a fruitful parent. Assuming I do, my kids will probably retaliate in their specific manner. I can rather attempt to shape myself. Normally kids take cues from us.

I can deal with valuing my kids for what their identity is and stress less over them. They will more likely come to see the value in themselves and have a less restless outlook on who they are, the point at which you can do this.

Once unwound, you will be quiet and sincerely separate to the point of directing your kid. You can then consider him responsible by giving results if he hasn't kept the guidelines or hasn't done what was generally anticipated of him. Do it unassumingly instead of with a lot of feeling. Separate assuming your kid has failed to keep a grip on himself. When he is quiet, you can examine with him different choices for tackling an issue, instead of shouting, hollering, and attempting to keep others prisoner. He will discover those specific ways of behaving are not viable because he just doesn't get what he needs when he acts in those negative ways. Also, you can show him better choices through your poise and critical thinking conversations. From your quiet separateness, you will want to direct your kid to a better way of behaving and a more serene year.

Chapter 4

Embarrassed about Your Kid's Behavior? Instructions to Cope with Judgment

At the point when your kid is pursuing unfortunate decisions and showcasing, it's not difficult to allow disgrace to gobble you up inside. You wonder, Where have I veered off-track as a parent? For what reason would he say he is acting along these lines? Also, What must others be thinking? The risk here is that these sentiments can make a negative cycle. At the point when you work out of dread and disgrace instead of out of clear objectivity and care for your kid not exclusively will you feel terrible, but you can likewise become incapable as a parent. If this sounds natural as it accomplishes for so many of us we should find out how you might break the cycle.

Disgrace: Lurking beneath the Surface

At the point when we're blissful, we giggle or feel a feeling of prosperity. At the point when we're irate or apprehensive, we get a shock of adrenaline. Yet, disgrace doesn't necessarily spread the word about itself rather, this damaging inclination will in general swim deep down. It tends to be depicted as that terrible inclination that causes you to feel as though every last one of your defects or downfalls as a parent is in plain view so anyone might be able to see. While we're feeling as such, we feel accused and decided by others regardless of whether they're just in our creative mind and we need to creep into an opening and vanish from sight.

It's vital to take note that disgrace is not the same as culpability. Culpability is what we feel when we don't act in manners that line up with our essential convictions and values. This could incorporate things like meddling or deceiving a friend or family member's trust. Disgrace, then again, isn't normally associated with a way of behaving, yet rather with who we accept we truly are. We can feel disgrace when we feel inept, shaky, excessively fat, or in some way or another loathsome. Disgrace is tied in with being, not tied in with acting two different things.
Here is the rub: You can feel disgrace about your defects, yet about others' ways of

behaving and these others are normally those nearest to you, similar to your kid or mate. I refer to this as "reflected disgrace. Here is a model. We should envision your young girl being in a tough situation constantly. She's gotten suspensions from school, takes part in medication and liquor use, and is transparently impolite of you and the different grown-ups in her life. You see different guardians attempting to get their children far from her due to her standing as a miscreant.

At the point when you stroll through town, you end up holding your head down and your eyes get some distance from individuals who could realize you are the mother of that delinquent young lady. You seldom mingle and end up going out less and now and again. Thus, you feel detached.

It's difficult to tell where you end and your kid starts. Disgrace, whether your own or from others, drives the profound anxiety toward not being generally adequate and not deserving of being adored.

Assuming you were the mother of the girl that I recently depicted, you would feel countless agonizing feelings other than disgrace: you would be stressed and apprehensive that your kid is acting in such damaging ways and you may resent her for making you look awful. You could fear for her future and have some culpability for previous mishaps you could have made as a parent. This multitude of feelings would impede your having the option to move toward your girl's issues in a quiet, smart way that could be useful to her to settle them.

Also, disgracing messages to guardians in our way of life are all over and it's hard for any parent not to retain them. Yet, regardless of whether we understand this, do we stop, delay and think under the steady gaze of we judge and inquire as to whether we concur with our convictions? Do we deliberately concur that we should be there to serve our children at whatever point and any way they need us, for instance? That we ought to have the option to control each move they make? More often than not we don't, yet we simply keep responding to these messages, a steady automatic dance that leaves us feeling hopeless, depleted, and "not sufficient.

Yet, here's how things are: our kid's way of behaving isn't a mirror mirroring a report card back to us of how we did as a parent. A parent's responsibility is to get a sense of ownership of their own decisions. You couldn't be liable for your kid's decisions; you can impact them, in any case, you have no control over them.

We can feel disgrace and fault ourselves with such ease on the off chance that we don't ponder what we accept or on the other hand assume our convictions even sound good to us. At times it's not even imaginable to sensibly live up to the assumptions society has set for us. Assuming your kid has ADHD, for instance, or regardless of whether he inspires him to stand by and act entirely constantly, it won't be sensible.

It's likewise vital to comprehend that disgrace makes more disgrace. The more we stow away from it and keep it in
obscurity, the greater it will develop. If you respond to your kid's unseemly or wild way of behaving by keeping away from social connections as many guardians do the more your tension will develop. You may be expecting that everybody in the city or your high rise is discussing the most recent caper that occurred with your kid. Large numbers of us at last begin inclination paranoid, as assuming everyone is focused on our loved ones. Also, honestly, individuals may be passing judgment on you, it's people's specialty. Yet, recall, you have no control over others' thought processes about you,

you can handle your opinion on yourself and how you answer them.
Things you can do when you're caught in the disgrace cycle as a parent and are prepared to get out of it.

Perceive the feeling of disgrace
It's difficult to recognize disgrace even though we are frequently determined by it without knowing it's there. A few hints that it's hiding on a deeper level incorporate ways of behaving like stowing away, staying away from, and bunches of mystery. Being excessively critical of yourself as well as other people is another hint that disgrace isn't far away.

At the point when you are cruelly passing judgment on yourself or others, stop
Stop to the point of inquiring as to whether what you are faulting and disgracing yourself for are convictions that you have gulped down from our way of life, or on the other hand assuming you genuinely concur

with them and decide to claim them. Ask yourself, do I truly concur that it's conceivable and sensible for me to ensure my kid never settles on an unfortunate decision in his life? Do I truly feel that it is workable for me to guarantee my youngster will constantly think how I figure he ought to? If the response is no, quit disgracing yourself. You could say, "I'm requesting that myself accomplish something that I disagree with and know is absurd. Furthermore, that doesn't check out.

Look at yourself

Take a gander at yourself and your own set of experiences to know why you are feeling such a lot of disgrace and frustration about your kid's way of behaving. Assuming there's an issue that is repeating something you went through previously and haven't yet dealt with, would you say you are as yet disgracing yourself now? Is it true or not that you are accidentally putting the profound feeling of your defects onto your kid? Typically, on the off chance that we will look carefully, genuinely at a circumstance, rather than over-zeroing in on our children, our unsettled circumstances will ascend to the top. If your youngster accomplishes something unpleasant like annihilating your neighbor's property or taking something, remind yourself, "It's not me, it's my kid. Presently how might I be useful and valuable to her in this present circumstance? What's the higher perspective here, and what example would I like to ensure she learns?

Remind yourself what you are answerable for

Advise yourself that you are just answerable for your way of behaving and to be the best parent, mate, companion, and little girl that you can be. You should show up for your kid in positive or negative times, get help when fundamental, and be a useful aide. Above all, continue to appear.

Surrender mysterious reasoning

Relinquish the otherworldly reasoning that says, If I could be the ideal parent, I could some way or another decide my youngster's way of behaving and feeling. That much command over someone else is essentially unrealistic. At the point when you can surrender that deception and reasonably realize what is conceivable, you will begin to feel less disgrace and quit accusing yourself. You will likewise be more ready to converse with different guardians and see that you're in good company by the way you think and feel.

Hold your head high

It could sound silly, but when you go out in broad daylight, hold your head high and visually engage. Although you could feel awful disgrace over your kid's way of behaving, you know not you did the medications, shoplifted, tormented somebody, or went with other disastrous decisions. You are not your kid; the umbilical string was cut quite some time in the past. Your trademark could need to be, I am not my youngster and my kid isn't me.

Judgment from others

At the point when others judge you or your kid, advise yourself that you have no control over how others see you yet you have some control over how you check out at yourself as well as other people. Individuals will pass judgment on you less assuming you quit hanging out. By telling them you, they will be more averse to faulting you. Most importantly you must be seen. Assuming they judge you, help yourself to remember the accompanying I have no control over how others view me. I can handle how I view myself and how I answer them.

Converse with nonjudgmental individuals who you can trust

The answer for diminishing your disgrace is outlandish: It is to move toward individuals and begin having contact with the rest of the world once more. Converse with individuals with whom you have a very valid justification to figure you can trust. Have a go at sharing a portion of your battles. Tell them what you're going through so their minds don't roam free. Who can say for sure, that they may be going through the same thing or have a niece, nephew, or colleague who is?

As you converse with others transparently, your disgrace will reduce because you will perceive that what you accept to be most dishonorable is generally human. Furthermore, when you feel more human and can relinquish a portion of the disgrace you feel, you'll have the option to move toward your kid from a smart spot, not an exceptionally close-to-home one. Really at that time could you at any point start to have a reasonable relationship with him, see him all the more plainly, and have the option to assist him with refocusing? From that place, you will want to be a significantly more viable parent which will prompt less disgrace about being an insufficient one.

Shouting at Your Kids? Why It Doesn't Work

You know the drill: Your kid is shouting at you, disregarding you, being reckless or frightful. Unexpectedly, you're hollering as loud as possible, matching him decibel for decibel. Afterward, you think, Why did I go bonkers once more? I'm so burnt out on allowing him to provoke me with such ease.

Hollering is a characteristic reaction when your children are impolite, not tuning in, participating in a reckless way of behaving, mistreating you, or in whatever other circumstance that sets off your feelings. Although you realize it would be better if you would remain cool-headed, it's difficult to genuinely consistently do that. Or on the other hand, you might try and contend that hollering and making our children terrified of us worked when we were growing up, so is there any good reason why we shouldn't do that today?

Hollering or losing it sends the message, "I want you to act so I can feel quieter. I don't have the foggiest idea how to be quiet and in charge of myself except if you are acting how I want you to. It was adequate for me

At the point when our folks were raising us, grown-ups utilized dangers, terrorizing, and dread to terrify us into a better way of behaving. The value was acquiescence. A few guardians hit and others pulled out affection to get their youngsters to submit to power. Furthermore, kids were substantially more submissive than the present children yet it included some significant downfalls. Albeit the present guardian's esteem dutifulness, we likewise put a high worth on long haul associations, cultivating freedom and confidence, building trust, and on our children's prosperity. The prior approach to nurturing could assist jokes around conforming, yet it neutralizes a portion of the present guardians' qualities.

So the inquiry becomes, How would we get our children to act without hollering and shouting, while likewise constructing a decent connection with them? It's memorable and critical that our terrible attitude might encourage us at the time. It's an approach to dealing with our pain however it doesn't feel improved later. It doesn't upgrade the relationship with our children that we desire to accomplish after some time or assist them with forming effectively into dependable grown-ups.

The message you send when you lose it.

There are numerous ways of impacting your youngster's way of behaving, yet hollering isn't powerful. The message that it communicates to our children is frequent. I'm confused. I don't have the foggiest idea of how to inspire you to act how I believe that you should act. I feel crazy. The message we maintain that our kids should get is, I'm in charge of myself. I understand what to do and you don't control me. Yelling or losing it likewise communicates the message, I want you to act so I can feel quieter. I don't have any idea how to be quiet and in charge of myself except if you are acting how I want you to. What happens is that your kid feels that he is responsible for your profound prosperity and that is not a decent situation to place him in.

Although we maintain that our kids should be independent and free in their reasoning, we are setting them up to act in response to us. This is the opposite of self-direction. Now your kid should either do what you want to quiet you down or conflict with what you want if he would rather not be accountable for your profound wellbeing. Neither one of the ways of behaving will assist your youngster with having an independent perspective, being independent, or gaining from the regular outcomes of his own decisions.

Chapter 5

How being calm changes the game

Keep in mind that tension and upset are infectious as is quiet. On the off chance that you can work quietly, you will help model for your children lifetime expertise that will assist them with doing great in their connections. Reward: when you perceive that you are not liable for definitive decisions that your kid makes, you will feel quieter and when you feel quieter, you will want to consider better nurturing techniques to assist your kid with pursuing better decisions.

A few different ways that will assist you with halting hollering while at the same time directing your kid toward additional helpful ways of behaving.

Contemplate what you are answerable for. Assuming you believe you're answerable for each choice and decision your kid makes, you will feel insufficient and restless, which will make you receptive. However, if you remember you couldn't be answerable for their decisions, you will quiet down and feel less restless. All things considered, remain accountable for what you are liable for and how you act when she is acting inadequately.

That is in your grasp. For instance, your youngster chooses to sneak a treat before supper, although he's not permitted. You're not liable for his decision, yet you are dependable to deal with your reactions smoothly and maturely and to consider how to assist him with keeping the guidelines that are set by giving him a ramification for his activities.

Know your triggers. Plan and get ready for your triggers. Assuming you get set off when your kid is impolite to you, get ready and plan what you will do other than shouting. You have options. Prepare how you will respond when set off so you will not be surprised. In that brief moment between the trigger occasion and your response to it, you have control. Plan your break. Go for a stroll, call a companion, stand by listening to music, put on earphones, sing, think, and relax. Deal with different challenges in your day-to-day existence so the pressure of those circumstances doesn't spill onto your youngster.

Genuinely promise to assume responsibility for your responses. Invest in assuming responsibility for your profound responses (and those triggers we were discussing) as opposed to investing that time into attempting to control your children. Perceive that by losing it you're requesting that your kids deal with you rather than you being the adult who no longer has hissy fits when others don't act how you need. By assuming responsibility for your triggers and responses, you will be in a superior situation to have your kids figure out how to act. Understand that your kid has the privilege to pick how to act regardless of whether it is a terrible decision you don't have command over their inclinations and decisions. Instead of being distraught at them, conclude how you can direct them to better perspectives by giving powerful outcomes. For instance, assuming that your kid continues neglecting to say thank you for Grandma's gift, as opposed to being distraught and hollering, conclude how he can learn.

Here is a reality he will learn better without the entirety of your emotionality. One potential result is that you don't permit him to have the gift until he sends, says, or composes a thank you to Grandma.

Perceive pressure in your life. Hollering can be demonstrative of how focused you are. Take a selfie-stock. Is it true or not that you are excessively centered around your kid's way of behaving because you are under-centered around your own life? Do you have to focus harder on your grown-up connections or your objectives? Perhaps you want to stand firm with your better half and his drinking. Or on the other hand, maybe you've been over-working for your untrustworthy sibling for a long time. Are these stressors making you spill a portion of this nervousness onto your kids? You could likewise be losing it regularly because your family is over-focused. Is your way of life excessively excited with every one of the timetables, requests, and exercises? We need our children dynamic, yet assuming we invest such a lot of energy going around, we will not possess energy for connections. Set aside some margin to thoroughly consider what is truly best for the family.

On the off chance that you can scale back things or supplant portions of your overbooked plan with something to everybody's greatest advantage (like spare energy, supper together a few times each week at least, and so on), there may be less pressure in the home.

Know your limits: Remaining quiet with your kid expects you to remain as genuinely separate from her as you can. Know where you end and she starts. At the point when you can be discreet, you will be in a superior situation to perceive the truth about her and you'll understand what you need to provide for her to act well. By doing this, you will be better ready to direct her.

Keep in mind, that closeness comes from separateness hollering truly is the

consequence of being excessively enmeshed. For instance, on the off chance that you stress that your high schooler isn't keeping up in that frame of mind, of letting her face the normal outcomes or setting stricter rules around homework time, you step in and begin finishing her schoolwork for her. This hazy spots the limits and doesn't allow her the opportunity to figure out how to use sound judgment all alone.
Being a quiet parent is vital to your wellbeing, and the strength of your family, as well as concerning every single great relationship. By not hollering and by keeping mentally collected and practical, you will be more valid and regarded by your kid, and in this manner all the more profoundly associated.

These are the large acquisitions that will assist you with remaining focused while you're accomplishing the difficult work of nurturing during your children's more youthful years and later when they're developed, you'll have a solid groundwork and structure whereupon to fabricate your grown-up relationship.

The most effective method to Not To Get Triggered by Kids' Misbehaviors

At the point when children get rowdy, it's more straightforward to fly off the handle than to put them down and talk. Particularly while they're rehashing a way of behaving that they've been told NOT to do. While many guardians grew up with furious drill sergeants for guardians, some chose to break the cycle. It's an intense fight to keep up with that beauty and balance as a parent. In any case, ideally, these tips will assist with holding one back from getting set off by their children's mischief.

Establishing

Not quite the same as establishing the children, establishing implies finding one item to hyperfocus on to keep the feelings from detonating when children get into mischief. This is likewise a typical adapting method utilized among those with tension particularly when contemplations go crazy. To ground oneself, inhale profound and center around one article and portray it comparable to the five detects. For instance, on the off chance that it's a blossom in the room, answer the accompanying inquiries:

Sight - What tone is the blossom?
Smell - What does the blossom resemble?
Taste - Is the blossom palatable?
Contact - Is the blossom delicate or thorny?
Hearing - Is there wind brushing the leaves around?
When the inquiries are responded to, feelings would have cooled off and it'll be simpler to deal with. It doesn't need to be in bloom. It can likewise be a toy or a shade, or any article inside the room.

Counting in reverse

A fan number one of the trigger plugs is counting in reverse. Shut your eyes, take a full breath, and consider 10 in reverse gradually as one can. To feel it more, it's alright to likewise genuinely make 10 strides back. Doing so permits one to accept that they have sincerely eliminated themselves from the circumstance, keeping the children's mischief from setting off things.

If 10 isn't sufficient, it's alright. Do one more arrangement of 10 until things cool off.

Mantra reciting

No, this isn't the stuff individuals say while thinking in yoga. Rehashing specific words that hold a specific load to one can likewise help with establishing and reviewing what sort of nurturing one should do. A mantra can be pretty much as straightforward as, solid, firm, and kind to persistently help one to remember the guarantee to be a delicate

parent. Take a virus drink before going through the discipline
On the off chance that alcohol is known as "fluid mental fortitude", cold water ought to be known as "fluid delicate discipline". At the point when an individual lashes out, their blood warms up, and the strain increments. Drinking some virus water can assist with dialing the blood and dropping the strain back to hold the trigger back from rising. At times, triggers can likewise be through stifling which the water can help ease

Deliberately keeping away from "warnings" of the triggers

Essentials to one's triggers may now and again be known as "warnings". These triggers frequently accompany an admonition. So it turns out to be not difficult to recognize the more careful one becomes. At the point when children transform into a "toy-nado", they habitually have cautioning sounds, for example, shouting, laser shooting sounds, blast audio cues, and different things. Here is a portion of the warnings of the various types of twisters kids make:

Tornado - Usually finished by babies, they shout a rallying call and get irregular toys before twirling around to throw them all over the place. They may likewise begin eating like a tuFashionado - Teens are well known for this particularly when they don't have anything to wear notwithstanding having a closet choice taking steps to pop. Its requirements incorporate teenagers yelling a few doors down, "Mother/ATE/YAYA, I CAN'T FIND MY (INSERT CLOTHing PIECE HERE)! HAVE YOU SEEN IT!?" and wild-eyed running all over the steps. That, or then again if there are sisters, plan for some shouting, for example, "Offer BACK MY CLOTHES!", "WHY ARE YOU USING MY FAVORITE SHIRT?", "Quit BORROWING MY STUFF!",

"Bruha ka!" and many, numerous different obscenities.

Food-nado - Pre-youngsters and adolescents who need to figure out how to cook are the typical eyes of this twister. While it's ideal to hear that they need to become familiar with the fundamental ability of cooking, triggers, for example, rattling pots and containers, the skipping of glass and fire, and a peculiar smell of some recipes can cause uneasiness. Most of the time, these typically happen at noon while they're getting a terrible instance of the munchies.

Staying away from these warnings can be through having separate clothing bushels per kid, assisting your school with joking, tracking down a modest spot to tie their readings, and utilizing the toys as a feature of the home stylistic layout.

Yet, assuming command over one's triggers towards children's mischievous activities can take time. There will be mistakes yet when one gets the tips down, things will be significantly more straightforward

www.ingramcontent.com/pod-product-compliance
Lightning Source LLC
LaVergne TN
LVHW050317160826
845677LV00014B/3436

* 9 7 9 8 8 4 7 9 3 1 1 4 4 *